The Hangry Cookbook

Susan Ray

Copyright © 2024 by Susan Ray/Discovering Home

All rights reserved.

No portion of this book may be reproduced in any form without written permission from the publisher or author, except as permitted by U.S. copyright law.

For Danielle in the morning
For Nick in the afternoon
And for Alan anytime
With love

and gratitude for your understanding and patience during the countless times I have been – just a little – hangry, too!

Contents

The Basics		1
1.	BREAKFAST	3
2.	Dawn's Early Light-ning Meal	5
3.	Monkeying Around Morning	7
4.	Morning Grouch-wich	9
5.	Mighty Milquetoast	11
6.	Running on Eggy	13
7.	Rising and Shining	15
8.	Oh-My-Lettes	17
9.	Nuts O'The Dough	19
10.	Stacking Up the Pancakes	21
11.	Fresh From the Tree Overnight Oatmeal	23
12.	LUNCH	25
13.	Chick -N- Greens	27

14.	Peanut Butter and …	29
15.	Row, Row, Row, Potato	31
16.	It's a Rare-Bit of Welsh	33
17.	Sunny Up Cover Up	35
18.	Flashy-French Onion Soup	37
19.	Presto Pizza	39
20.	Surf and Verte	41
21.	Kinda Sorta Grilled Cheese	43
22.	A Cuppa Cheer	45
23.	DINNER	47
24.	Now and Later Soup	49
25.	Kitchen Sink Delight	51
26.	Pork Berry	53
27.	Smooshed Potatoes	55
28.	Deli Dinner	57
29.	Mere Minutes 'til Meatloaf	59
30.	Too Hot to Cook	63
31.	Chicken Can Do	65
32.	Fishing for Compliments	67
33.	Craving Cornbread	69
34.	DESSERTS	71
35.	Yo-Gurt to Like This Banana Split	73
36.	What Cookies?	75
37.	Par-Fancy and Par-Fast	77

38.	Thanks for the Cake	79
39.	Yo-PB-Freeze	81
40.	Oh, Sweet Milquetoast	83
41.	S'mores Weather	85
42.	Beyond Pudding	87
43.	Snap Your Fingers Fudge	89
44.	Chip-A-Roo Bars	91
45.	Nothing New No-Bakes	93
46.	Recipes for Recipes	97
	A Note to the Reader	101
47.	But wait, there's more ...	103

The Basics

Hello fellow grumpy, hungry person!

I imagine that you and I are similar in many ways, namely being less than delightful company when we are in serious need of something, anything to devour!

Well, this cookbook is designed for those ravenous, cranky, there is nothing to eat, ARGH moments. It might not be the cookbook you grab when you want to impress a date with your culinary prowess, but it can be a handy tool when you want sustenance. And you want it now.

Before you get too excited, though, I have to be honest with you. These recipes were created with the understanding that you do have a reasonable inventory of food, as in real food, in your kitchen. No, you don't need to dash out and buy artisan cheeses or invest in imported chocolates (although both sound pretty good right now), but you will need to keep some staples like flour, fresh or frozen veggies, and yogurt on hand.

You will also need a basic knowledge of cooking and baking. We aren't going to make a cassoulet, but we will do more than reheat canned soup. If you can cut up veggies without having a medical team on standby, and you know the difference between simmering and boiling, then your time spent being hangry will be reduced and your kitchen will become your happy, or maybe just happier, place.

I'll share one last important thought with you: When possible, piggyback your prep work and your cooking. What I mean by that is when scrambling eggs for breakfast, beat up another egg or two, dip some bread into the mixture and cook up a little French toast for the following morning. Plain, unbuttered, syrup-free French toast can be tossed into a tightly sealed plastic baggie and frozen, then popped into a toaster whenever you feel *faim*!

The same is true for ground meats. When browning ground beef or pork for tacos, save a little cooked, but unseasoned meat for another meal. It freezes well, thaws quickly, and can be tossed into canned soup, on top of a frozen pizza, or stirred into store bought spaghetti sauce for added protein. Eating good food fast is quicker and easier when you piggyback the preparation and the cooking than if you have to start at square one every time you walk into the kitchen.

I hope these recipes do more than offer speedy meals that taste good. I hope they encourage you to play with ingredients, discover new food combinations, and see cooking less as a chore and more as a respite.

So, without further ado, let's begin!

BREAKFAST

Dawn's Early Light-ning Meal

This is obviously a healthy breakfast, but when using frozen berries in particular, it can be enjoyed as a dessert!

- 2 large spoonfuls plain Greek yogurt
- Honey, local if possible
- 1 Tablespoon each chia seeds, flax seeds, etc. (optional, but they contribute nicely to the flavor)
- 1/2 to 1 cup berries, unsweetened, frozen or fresh
- Nuts: Walnuts, almonds, pecans, etc.

In a big cereal bowl, blend the honey into the yogurt. Add the seeds, grains and mix well.

Top with the fruit and toss on some nuts.

Monkeying Around Morning

Mmmm, the idea of banana pancakes sounds so good, but do you have enough time to stand in line at one of those mega-pancake places? Why not hang out at home with a bunch of these instead?

- 2 bananas, nicely ripe
- 4 eggs
- 1 cup flour: All purpose, whole wheat, buckwheat, etc. work well
- 1 teaspoon baking powder
- 1 teaspoon vanilla extract
- 1 1/2 teaspoons cinnamon

In a large bowl, mash the bananas well before adding the eggs. Mix thoroughly.

In a separate bowl, stir together the dry ingredients before adding to the banana mixture, a little at a time. Then mix in the vanilla extract and cinnamon.

Heat the skillet to medium-low before spooning 1/4 cup of the batter into the pan. Cook until bubbles start to form and pop on the surface, then flip each pancake and cook only until the surface is smooth to the touch.

Beware that the high sugar content of these pancakes will speed up the browning process, so watch them carefully.

>If you have the time, pancakes are fluffier if the batter rests in the fridge for 10-30 minutes, but don't worry about this extra step. They are still delicious even if you cook them right away.

Morning Grouch-Wich

This is really just a morning egg salad without the mixing! You can always serve this as an afternoon salad by ignoring the bread, or you could serve it as a dip for crackers or raw veggies.

- 2 slices bread, toasted
- 1 hard boiled egg, sliced or smooshed with a fork
- Tomato, sliced or chopped
- Handful of raw greens (spinach, lettuce, etc.)
- Onion, thinly sliced
- Mayonnaise or plain Greek yogurt, to taste
- Mustard, to taste
- Celery seed
- Shake of salt or salt-substitute
- Dash of ground pepper

Compile your breakfast sandwich by spreading mayo, yogurt, mustard, whatever you'd like on your toast. Then cover one slice of toast with tomato, greens and onion slices. Use a fork to gently smoosh your hard boiled egg onto the second slice, or put that handy egg slicer gadget to work instead! Put both sides together and press lightly; cut into quarters for easy eating while looking for your keys, those papers you just had in your hand, and downing the last gulp of coffee.

>Grabbing some of last night's leftover salad is a speedier option than slicing or tearing greens in the morning. And it's easy to add any odds and ends that have been snoozing in your fridge:

avocado slices
guacamole
green pepper
cooked, crumbled bacon
salsa
assorted cheeses
olives, pickles
hot sauce

Mighty Milquetoast

A traditionally soothing dish named for Harold T. Webster's comic strip character, Casper Milquetoast, from 1924.

2 slices best quality bread
2 cups whole milk, ideally, but any other milks are fine, too
Butter
Salt
Pepper

While toasting the bread to a lovely golden brown, gently heat the milk over low heat in a saucepan on the stove. Stir frequently and do not allow it to scorch.

When the toast is done, spread generously with butter, cut into bite-sized pieces, and place in a bowl. Cover with warmed milk and sprinkle with salt and pepper. Serve immediately.

>If you'd like something less ... Milquetoast-esque ... just top with grated cheese. And diced onion. And chopped ham. The possibilities are endless, but once you add snazzy ingredients, the whole Milquetoast experience is no more. You will have created some kind of milk and bread soufflé without the rise? No matter what, it will be soothing stuff.

Running on Eggy

This is a 100% reliable method for making soft boiled eggs. Delicious with hot, buttered toast, and oh so elegant served in a vintage egg cup. Just be sure to use a ruler and a timer.

1 cold, just from the fridge, raw egg, in its shell
1/2 inch of water (Please note that this is how deep the water will be in the pot, not in a measuring cup.)
2 or 4 quart saucepan with a lid

Bring the 1/2" of water to a boil.
Carefully place the egg into the boiling water.
Put the lid on the pan.
Turn the heat down to low.
Leave the egg undisturbed for 6 1/2 minutes exactly.
Remove the egg from the pan and tah dah! You have a perfectly cooked soft boiled egg!

Rising and Shining

I have to admit that I experimented with a plethora of super-quick biscuit recipes, my own and others', that promised a lot, but delivered inedible and sometimes freakish bread-like patties of mystery. This is the only recipe that is worth your time.

2 cups Martha White self rising flour (White Lilly is OK, too, but Martha is the best option.)

1/4 cup shortening (Or even better, lard. Seriously better.)

1 cup buttermilk (Whole milk is fine, but buttermilk makes it taste mmmmm.)

Preheat the oven to 450* Line baking sheets with parchment paper.

In a large bowl, use a pastry cutter, two knives, a fork, and/or your hands to be sure the shortening/lard is evenly distributed. You are aiming for a coarse meal of shortening and flour.

Add the buttermilk and stir with a fork. Not a spoon. You want to mix it just until it is combined, not smoosh all of the shortening as if you were creaming it.

When you have a sticky dough, plop it onto a lightly dusted surface and knead it for less than a minute. Fold it over, knead it into itself, turn the dough, fold it over, knead it into itself ... do this about seven times.

Now you can roll it out, about 1" thick, and use a round cutter or a floured rim of a glass to cut out the biscuits. Be sure to cut straight down. Don't twist until you reach the bottom of the dough, or else your biscuits will tilt when baking.

Or you can be like me and simply pull off equal-sized balls of the dough, patting them a little to flatten them out.

Place the neat or sloppy biscuits on the prepared pans, close to, but not touching one another. Bake for 9-11 minutes, until they are that lovely golden brown on top.

These biscuits don't require much more time than many other "quick" recipes, and the result is amazing. And you can freeze them, use them for strawberry shortcakes, or fill with ham and cheese for a fast sandwich later.

Oh-My-Lettes

These are such fluffy and delicious omelets, it's almost a shame to add anything to them. But go ahead and add to them with wild abandon! You just can't go wrong with this recipe!

   1 Tablespoon butter for the pan
   2 eggs
   1 teaspoon vanilla extract
   Splash of milk for richer omelets OR Splash of water for lighter omelets
   2 Tablespoons uncooked pancake batter

In a medium bowl, whisk the eggs, vanilla, and liquid of choice. Whisk rapidly in order to incorporate as much air as possible into the mixture. Right before cooking, whisk the raw pancake batter into the eggs.

Melt the butter in the skillet, heat it until the butter foams but does not brown.

Pour the egg mixture all at once into the heated pan. Tilt the pan to allow the liquid to run into the empty spaces.

Cook until the mixture begins to set, then gently loosen the edges, allowing the last of the liquid egg mixture to move to the outer edge.

Cook just until there is a hint of liquid in the center of the omelet. Add any fillings at this point, if desired.

Slide the omelet onto a warm plate, folding as you pull the pan away. The egg will continue to cook once it is folded over.

Enjoy!

Nuts O'The Dough

When frying anything, be sure to watch the temperature of your oil: Too cold, and you'll have grease-osities. Too hot, and you will end up with a doughy mess on the inside and crust on the outside!

Baking Mix Wonders
3 cups baking mix (Bisquick, Jiffy, etc.)
1 cup milk
Peanut or vegetable oil, to be used for frying

In a large bowl, stir the baking mix and the milk together to make a dough. Let it rest as you heat the oil.

Begin by heating 4" of oil in a deep frying pan or a Dutch oven. You'll want the temperature of the oil to remain between 350* to 360*

Carefully drop the dough by spoonfuls into the heated oil, only two or three at a time. Use tongs to turn each one over to ensure both sides are golden brown.

Scoop the cooked doughnut drops out with a slotted spoon and allow to drain on a rack and blot with paper towels. While still warm, toss in granulated or powdered sugar, or cinnamon and sugar, or dip into melted chocolate.

Refrigerated Dough Wonders
1 can refrigerated biscuit dough, 10 count size
Peanut or vegetable oil, to be used for frying

Use a small cookie cutter or sharp knife to cut out a circle from the middle of each biscuit.

In hot oil (see temperature information above), carefully lower one to three rings into the pan or Dutch oven.

These will cook quickly, in about one minute!

When golden brown on both sides, use a slotted spoon to remove the donuts carefully.

Don't forget to fry those "doughnut holes", too!

Allow to drain on rack and blot with paper towels, then cover in sugar, cinnamon and sugar, powdered sugar, etc. while still hot.

Oh my! So good – and very fresh!

Stacking Up the Pancakes

If you have a chance to visit a maple syrup farm, try some Grade B syrup (AKA Dark, Robust), still hot and fresh from the evaporator. I think that it has a richer, more satisfying flavor than the lovely, but less delightful, amber colored Grade A.

- 1 cup all-purpose flour
- 1/2 cup granulated sugar
- 1/2 cup brown sugar
- 3 teaspoons baking powder
- 1/4 teaspoon salt
- 1 egg
- 1/2 cup buttermilk or plain Greek yogurt
- 1 Tablespoon vanilla extract
- 2 tablespoons melted butter

1/4 cup soda, ginger ale is best (This makes the pancakes especially light and fluffy.)

In a small mixing bowl, stir together the dry ingredients, set aside.

In a large bowl, blend the egg, buttermilk, vanilla, and melted butter. Add the flour mixture and stir to blend before adding the ginger ale. It is perfectly OK to have some lumps in the batter.

Cover the bowl with plastic wrap and place in the refrigerator for 15 minutes.

Remove from fridge, stir once or twice.

>You may want to reserve 2 tablespoons of batter for the Oh-My-Lettes recipe.

Spoon batter into a hot pan, cooking until bubbles form and pop on the surface, then flip each pancake and cook only until the surface is smooth to the touch.

Enjoy these pancakes immediately, or allow to cool and refrigerate after separating each pancake between sheets of waxed paper.

Fresh From the Tree Overnight Oatmeal

You don't need to wait for cold weather to enjoy this warming oatmeal, and that's a great thing because eating such a robust breakfast is a terrific way to begin any day.

- 4 cups water or milk, or a combination
- 1 cup stone cut oats
- 1 teaspoon cinnamon
- 1/2 teaspoon each: ginger, cloves, nutmeg
- 3 apples, cored, quartered and grated
- Nuts, raw or roasted

Pour the water/milk/combo into a slow cooker. Add the uncooked stone cut oats and stir to evenly distribute. Cook on LOW overnight.

Add the shredded apple about 30 minutes before serving, or simply stir into each bowl as it is being dished up.

In the morning, spoon out a generous helping of the cooked oatmeal, then stir in the spices and top with nuts.

>The remaining oatmeal can be reheated in the microwave with a little milk, or stirred cold into yogurt for added fiber and protein.

LUNCH

Chick-N-Greens

This recipe is hearty enough for a meal, yet light enough for a side dish, depending upon the portion size. It can be made ahead and refrigerated in separate containers, or taken for lunch in just one bowl. Top with a handful of slivered almonds for added crunch.

- 1 cup plain Greek yogurt or mayonnaise
- 2 Tablespoons lemon juice
- 1 teaspoon garlic powder
- 1 teaspoon chives
- 1 teaspoon dill
- 2 cups cooked chicken, chopped (Rotisserie, canned, any leftover chicken will work.)
- 2/3 cup celery
- 1/3 cup onion, chopped
- 1/2 cup cooked (canned) white beans, rinsed and drained

Generous portion mixed greens

In a small bowl, whisk together the yogurt/mayonnaise, lemon juice, garlic and herbs. You might want to use a blender or immersion blender instead of a whisk for a very smooth, emulsified result. Set aside.

In a second bowl, toss the chicken with the celery, onion and beans.

When ready to serve, place a mound of fresh, mixed greens on a plate, top with the chicken mixture, then drizzle with the yogurt/mayonnaise dressing.

Peanut Butter and ...

We all know about PB&Js, and some of us adore PB&B (banana), but there are many other tasty ways to enjoy peanut butter any time of the day.

PB Hummus – seriously!

2 cups canned garbanzo beans, well drained

1/4 cup broth, veggie or chicken

1/4 cup lemon juice (lime is a nice alternative)

1 teaspoon garlic powder, or 2 Tablespoons fresh garlic, minced

1/4 cup nut butter: peanut, cashew, etc.

1 Tablespoon olive oil

Combine all of these ingredients in a food processor and voila! Grab the chips, spread it on a slice of bread, or save time and just grab a spoon!

A Few Additional Ideas!

If you are too hungry to wait for the whirl of the food processor, just add a dollop of nut butter to these tasty options:

- ... apple slices
- ... maple syrup
- ... cheddar cheese slices
- ... celery
- ... hot oatmeal
- ... chocolate
- ... sweet potato
- ... blueberries
- ... crackers
- ... plain yogurt
- ... bacon
- ... ice cream
- ... pancakes
- ... pretzels
- ... and with ginger and lime for a salad dressing

Row, Row, Row, Potato

What are sometimes called Potato Boats are perfect as a full meal or a side dish. This is a lifesaving recipe when you need something hot and filling on the double!

1 potato per person, good sized russets are best
Butter
Cream or milk
Plain yogurt and/or sour cream
Cooked bacon, crispy and drained
Chives
Shredded cheese

Wash, but do not peel each potato. Carefully poke all over with the tines of a fork to allow the steam to escape.

Wet paper towels, wringing all of the excess water from them before lightly wrapping each raw potato in this damp covering.

Microwave the potatoes using your microwave's setting, or 5-7 minutes, before testing for doneness. That is done by gently pressing the sides of the cooked potato. You want it to feel evenly pliant, soft, but not like complete mush inside. If needed, microwave again in 1-2 minute intervals.

Remove the hot potato from the microwave, slice it open lengthwise, then scoop out most of the cooked interior. Leave enough of a wall to prevent the potato from completely collapsing. Place the scooped potato innards into a bowl.

Add some butter, cream/milk, and a little yogurt/sour cream to the potato, then blend well. Make sure all of the ingredients are well combined and almost smooth.

At this point, you can stir in the chives, bacon, etc., or use those as toppings.

Refill each potato with generous amounts of this mixture, then pop into the microwave for a minute or two, or place in a hot oven, even under a broiler, if you'd like a toasty brown top.

Serve with shredded cheese, and maybe a spoonful of yogurt/sour cream on top.

It's a Rare-Bit of Welsh

Often called Welsh Rarebit or sometimes, Welsh Rabbit, this cheesy, rich, piping hot meal is just the thing on a snowy day. But never fear, no bunnies will be harmed in the making of this centuries old dish.

1/2 pound extra sharp cheddar cheese, diced or shredded

1 Tablespoon butter

1/2 teaspoon dried mustard, or 1 teaspoon of prepared

Pepper, black or cayenne, to taste

1 egg, beaten

1/2 cup beer: the better the quality, the better the result

4 slices best quality bread, toasted just before serving

In a heavy pan, or on top of a double boiler, combine the cheese, butter, mustard, pepper. Stir constantly and cook over low heat just until the cheese has melted nicely.

In a heat-proof bowl, slowly add a small amount of the hot mixture to the beaten egg, taking your time so the egg doesn't curdle. Whisk to combine.

Incorporate the egg and cheese blend into the original cheese mixture in the pan. Add salt if desired.

Add the beer and cook for another 2 minutes, stirring frequently. You want the rarebit to be well combined and hot, but do not boil.

Spoon over toast and enjoy, but note that this is very rich, so adjust your portions accordingly.

Sunny Up Cover Up

F ried eggs always seem so breakfast-y, but they are an easy solution to midday hunger pangs, as well. Just don't overheat your pan, use as thin a spatula as possible to protect those tender yolks, and you'll end up with a great meal in minutes!

  2 eggs
  1/4 cup butter for frying, possibly more
  1/2 cup salsa
  1 teaspoon cilantro
  1/2 teaspoon cumin
  Pinch of coriander
  Dash of hot sauce, optional
  Cheese, sliced or shredded (Mexican pre-blend, extra sharp cheddar, etc.)
  Dollop (or more) plain Greek yogurt and/or sour cream
  2 slices hot toast

Begin by putting the bread slices into the toaster, but do not toast it yet.

Next, carefully break each egg into its own small bowl, or a tea cup, even a measuring cup. This method usually prevents a broken yolk, and makes slipping the raw egg into the hot skillet a little easier and smoother.

Set the bowls of raw eggs aside while you stir the salsa and herbs (and optional hot sauce) together in another small bowl. Set that to the side, as well.

Over medium heat, melt the butter, but do not allow it to foam or brown. Carefully, gently, pour/slide the eggs, one at a time from their containers to the heated pan.

Turn the heat to medium low and drop the toast into the toaster.

Focusing on the eggs, gently spoon the melted butter over each egg. When the yolks are still runny, but the white is set, gently slip a thin spatula beneath each egg and place on the hot toast.

Cover the hot egg with cheese, then top with the salsa mixture and a touch of plain Greek yogurt or sour cream.

Flashy-French Onion Soup

With cheese, bread, broth and thinly sliced onion, a rainy day can transform into an afternoon in Paris! And this recipe can take you there in about 30 minutes!

- 2 onions, medium sized
- 1/4 cup (1 stick) butter
- 1 1/2 cups beef broth, hot
- 1 1/2 cups chicken broth, hot
- 1 cup white wine
- 1 1/2 teaspoons Worchester sauce, adjust to taste
- French or Italian bread, Stale is great, or you can toast fresh
- Shredded cheeses (Gruyere is traditional, but Swiss or other light cheese will be fine!)

Slice the onions as thinly as possible, then put them into a large microwave safe bowl along with the butter. Microwave this for six minutes.

Add the broth (You can use any combination, or opt for water and dry onion soup mix.) and the wine, then microwave for another five minutes.

Lower the power setting to 50%, then stir and cook a little longer, about 20 minutes.

While the liquid base is cooking, tear the bread into bite sized pieces and place in each bowl. When cooked, ladle the broth and onion mixture into each bowl, topping with the shredded cheese.

You can always zap each bowl if you'd like the cheese to thoroughly melt. Serve nice and hot!

Presto Pizza

Who doesn't crave pizza when feeling a little, shall we say, cranky? This stovetop version doesn't require any patience, is packed with protein, and tastes, well, like you've stepped into a cheesy pizzeria (in a good way)!

2 cups shredded cheese, mozzarella, sharp cheddar, parmesan, etc.
Tomato, ripe and diced
Italian seasonings (oregano, basil, marjoram, etc.)
Mushrooms, cleaned and thinly sliced
Spinach leaves, clean and torn
Additional cheese, shredded or mini-balls of mozzarella

> Because this is a very thin pizza, be judicious in the amount of toppings you use. All of the ingredients need to be heated through.

Preheat a skillet (use a 10-12-inch diameter pan for best results) over medium heat. When warmed, sprinkle the shredded cheese evenly in the skillet, and allow to cook for 2-4 minutes, watching the edges carefully.

Add the prepared toppings, distributing them evenly, but leaving a margin around the outer edge to act as the crust . Cook another 2 or 3 minutes on low, until the toppings bubble and the edges are just crispy, golden-brown.

Slip the pizza onto a heat proof cutting surface and allow to set/cool for a minute or so.

Slice and devour. Try to share.

Surf and Verte

Do you dream of a refreshingly simple lunch, but are drowning in colorless and boring drive-through fare? Here is an afternoon option that is healthy, easy, and light.

- 1 handful of mixed greens
- 1 small onion, finely chopped or thinly sliced
- 1 small carrot, shredded
- 1/2 cup canned white beans, rinsed and drained
- 1/2 can of tuna, well drained and flaked
- 1 teaspoon lemon juice
- 1 teaspoon olive oil
- Dash of black pepper
- Splash of hot sauce, optional

In a large bowl, toss the greens, onion, carrot, beans and tuna together. Set aside.

In a very small bowl, whisk together the lemon juice and the olive oil, adding black pepper and hot sauce to taste, if at all.

Drizzle the dressing over the mixed greens mixture right before eating.

Kinda Sorta Grilled Cheese

Rainy days and chilly winds make tomato soup and grilled cheese sandwiches especially tempting, but what if you don't want to mess about with the frying and the turning and the watching and the burnt bread and all of that marvelous cheese escaping from the sides?

2 slices bread of choice
Slices of cheese: American, smoked gouda, Havarti, Swiss, etc.
Optional mustard, mayo

Toast the bread while slicing the cheese.
Add cheese, and optional spreads, between the slices of toasted bread and place on a microwave safe plate, then pop into the microwave.

Within 30- 60 seconds, you have a tidy grilled cheese. If you are like me and love a slice of tomato and maybe a touch of thinly sliced onion, as well, simply open the oozing deliciousness and slip the veggies right into the middle of your sandwich.

Easy peasy and not so greazy!

A Cuppa Cheer

W ithin minutes, you can have a cuppa cheer full of protein and a couple of veggies, too.

1/2 slice bread, torn into pieces
1/4 teaspoon plus a little extra olive oil
2 Tablespoons onion, diced (or a teaspoon of onion powder)
2 Tablespoons tomato, chopped (salsa works well, too)
2 Tablespoons crumbled bacon, cooked and crisp
Italian seasonings, to taste
1 egg
1/2 cup milk
Vanilla extract, just a drop
Cheese, shredded or a slice
A large microwave-safe mug

Rub the inside of the mug with just a little olive oil

In a small bowl, toss together the prepared bread, tomato, onion, bacon, 1/4 tsp. of olive oil, and seasonings until well mixed

Place in the mug, filling no more than 1/2 full.

In that now empty, small bowl, whisk the egg and milk together, adding just a drop of vanilla extract. Pour over the bread mixture, filling the mug no more than 2/3.

Place in the microwave and cook for 60 seconds. You want to see the liquid bubble up, but not spill over the rim of the mug. Allow it to rest in the microwave for 15 seconds, then microwave again for 30-60 seconds. You know the strength of your microwave, so adjust the time accordingly. You want the contents to be set in the very center, that is, not soupy at all.

When set and still hot, you can top it with some shredded cheese, giving the mug another quick zap in the microwave to melt that cheese beautifully.

DINNER

Now and Later Soup

Although this soup does get even better with slow simmering, if you need something to eat right away, it can be hot and ready in under 30 minutes.

1 jar marinara sauce (or a jar of pasta sauce, or cans of plain tomato sauce)

1 carton (4 cups) broth: veggie, chicken, beef

1 12-oz can tomatoes: stewed and chopped or fire roasted

2 packages frozen mixed vegetables (California Blend and Peas & Carrots work well.)

2 teaspoons garlic powder

2 Tablespoons Italian seasoning

Dash of pepper

2 teaspoons vinegar (red wine vinegar is best)

2 whole bay leaves > Be sure to remove these before serving

Gather your ingredients and plop everything into a large pot. A stock pot is a good choice if you have one. Stir to combine.

Over medium-high heat bring the soup to a boil. Allow it to cook for 5 minutes, stirring often. Reduce the heat to low and simmer for at least 10 minutes, ideally for 30.

Serve with a generous helping of crusty French bread!

Kitchen Sink Delight

A family favorite that we refer to as, "Atomic Waste", this dish is as versatile as it is quick. Have fun with it by adding ingredients or leaving some out.

1 pound lean ground beef
1 green pepper, rinsed, seeded and chopped
1 small can mushrooms, drained and roughly chopped
1 teaspoon garlic powder
1 Tablespoon onion powder
1/4 teaspoon black pepper
2 Tablespoons Italian seasoning
2 teaspoons Mrs. Dash mesquite, or other brand salt-free mesquite
1 can cream of celery soup
1 15-ounce can tomato sauce
1 cup dry egg noodles
Cheese: American and parmesan

Brown the ground beef in a large cooking pot over medium high heat. When cooked, remove the meat to a separate dish before cooking the prepared pepper in the drippings. When the pepper is almost done, stir in the mushrooms and seasonings.

Add the ground beef back to the pot and stir in the soup and tomato sauce.

Before adding the noodles, check the amount of liquid in the pot. Add water or broth as needed, then gently stir in the dry noodles.

Cover pot and reduce temperature to low. Allow to simmer while the noodles are cooking, about 12 minutes.

Stir in the cheese for a creamy soup, or ladle into bowls first, topping with cheese right before serving. Enjoy!

Pork Berry

Nice enough to serve to guests, but speedy enough for a weeknight meal, this quick and easy dish brings together the earthiness of pork with the brightness of cranberries.

- 4 boneless pork chops, about 4 ounces each
- 1 teaspoon sage
- 1 teaspoon thyme
- 1/4 teaspoon salt
- 1/4 teaspoon black pepper
- 2 Tablespoons and 1 Tablespoon butter
- 1/2 cup whole cranberry sauce, canned is fine
- 2 teaspoons balsamic vinegar
- 1 teaspoon dried rosemary, crushed
- 1 teaspoon onion powder
- 1/2 cup low salt broth, chicken or beef

Preheat the oven to 200* prior to cooking the pork chops.

Stir the sage, thyme, salt and black pepper together in a small bowl. Rinse and pat dry the raw pork chops before rubbing seasoning mixture all over the chops. Set aside.

Melt the 2 tablespoons of butter in a large skillet over medium-high heat, cook the boneless pork chops about 3-4 minutes per side, until the internal temperature reaches 140*.

Place cooked pork chops in an oven safe dish to keep warm in the oven. Cover to prevent them from drying out.

In a medium saucepan on top of the stove, whisk together the drippings from the skillet, 1 tablespoon butter, cranberry sauce, rosemary, onion, balsamic vinegar, and broth over medium-high heat. Allow to boil for 6 minutes, allowing it to reduce, stirring constantly.

Remove from the heat and let rest for 1-2 minutes. It will continue to thicken as it cools.

When ready to serve, spoon the sauce over each pork chop and serve with rice and a side of winter veggies.

Smooshed Potatoes

Even though boiling potatoes doesn't take a lot of time, when you have a tight schedule, saving a minute here and there really adds up. Try this side dish with the Mere Minutes Meatloaf, zap some frozen veggies, and you'll actually have time to enjoy your meal, not just cook it!

4 medium yellow potatoes, unpeeled, cleaned and pierced with the tines of a fork
Damp paper towels
1/4 cup butter, very soft but not melted
2 Tablespoons plain Greek yogurt and/or sour cream
Splash of milk or heavy cream
1 teaspoon garlic powder
Dash of salt and pepper

Wrap each pierced potato loosely in a damp paper towel. Pop into the microwave for 3-5 minutes, depending upon the size of the potatoes and the strength of your microwave. When pliant to the touch, discard the paper towels. Drop the cooked potatoes into a large bowl.

Smoosh the potatoes with a masher or heavy spoon, stirring in the butter, yogurt, sour cream, milk, garlic powder and salt and pepper until well blended. You could use an electric mixer for this step, too.

Serve nice and hot with the entrée of your choice.

>These reheat well the following day in the microwave with just a touch of milk and a quick stir.

Deli Dinner

Almost all of us have done it. We've gone to the grocery store hungry, if not actually hangry. And we've stopped at the deli for one-quarter pound of sliced provolone. Nothing more. Somehow, a virtual tower of those slippery, sliding baggies of deli cheeses and meats has taken over the shopping cart. Well, that makes tonight's dinner easy, anyway.

1 pound deli roast beef
2 Tablespoons butter
2 tablespoons all-purpose flour
4 cups beef broth
2 teaspoons garlic powder
1 teaspoon onion powder
1 Tablespoon Worcester sauce (optional, but it adds depth and saltiness)
Bread, thickly sliced and toasted

Leftover mashed potatoes

In a 4-cup measuring cup, or similarly sized bowl, stir the garlic and onion powders and the Worcester sauce into the beef broth. Set aside.

In a skillet heated to medium-high, melt the butter and sprinkle in the flour evenly. Use a whisk to stir the butter and flour mixture together to make a roux. You are actually cooking the flour, so this mixture needs to turn a little brown and to smell nutty. It takes about three minutes or so.

Reduce the heat to low and add the beef broth about a half cup at a time, whisking the entire time. When all of the broth has been incorporated into the roux, continue to cook and whisk until it is a little less thick than you'd like it to be. The gravy will thicken when it is removed from the heat.

Heat the leftover mashed potatoes (or use the Smooshed Potatoes recipe) in the microwave. Arrange the deli roast beef on the thick slices of bread, add a couple scoops of potatoes, then cover everything with the hot gravy.

Serve with a salad and veggie and you have a hearty meal in far less time than it would take to choose, much less slow roast, an eye of round!

Mere Minutes 'til Meatloaf

Few recipes are as personal as meatloaf recipes. Some people never use ketchup. Someone else refuses to add oatmeal. But no matter the ingredients, it can take an hour or more to cook this classic dish. The secret to this particular variation has nothing to do with ingredients and everything to do with ... pans.

2 pounds ground beef, the leaner the better
1 pound Italian sausage
2 eggs
1 cup old fashioned oatmeal, maybe a little more
1 cup tomato sauce OR 1/2 sauce and 1/2 ketchup
1 Tablespoon Worcester sauce
1 Tablespoon prepared mustard OR 2 teaspoons dry mustard
2 Tablespoons Italian seasoning

2 teaspoons black pepper

The first step is to spritz a little non-stick spray into each muffin tin cup, or simply use cupcake liners. This recipe can make 24-30 mini meatloaves, depending upon the size of your tins and how you fill them. Once you have pr3pared the tins, set the pans aside.

In a large mixing bowl, mash, squish, stir the ground meats together. A potato masher or a dough hook on a mixer can really help in the process. (According to Julia Childs, your clean, bare hands are the best tool for the job. I do this, but wear food service gloves over my hands.)

Next incorporate the eggs, ketchup and mustard, then the herbs and seasonings. Once all of the ingredients are evenly distributed, add the oatmeal, about a cup at a time. You'll need to check for any dry streaks since you are going for a cohesive mass.

At this point, adjust the liquid to dry ratio. If the concoction looks too wet, add just a little oatmeal. If it is falling apart and you cannot form a ball with it, add an egg. If it is just a little dry, add more tomato sauce or ketchup.

Preheat your oven to 350*

When the mixture is thoroughly combined, use an ice cream scoop, a measuring cup, or a spoon to place relatively equal amounts in each muffin tin. Fill each cup to no more than 2/3 full.

Top with a little squirt of ketchup if you'd like, or leave bare.

Bake at 350* for 30-35 minutes. If the tops begin to brown too quickly, cover loosely with aluminum foil, but most of the time, that is not necessary.

The internal temperature for ground meat needs to reach 160*F.

Remove from the oven carefully and wow – you have made meatloaf in about half the time required for a full loaf pan or two.

Some of the many benefits of using muffin tins, beyond the much shorter cooking time, are that you can slice these meatloaf muffins in half to make sliders, you now have meatballs for spaghetti night, and these are easy to freeze and simple to defrost in just the right quantity.

>The listed measurements for the herbs and seasonings are simply a suggestion. You'll want to adjust the amounts for your preferences and spice inventory.

Too Hot to Cook

Ahhh. Summertime. Lakes and ice cream and festivals and picnics and ... heat. And humidity. And little interest in using the stove, much less the oven. Never fear! This is a satisfyingly cool recipe that can be made ahead in sections, then compiled right at the table.

4 cans tuna, packed in water and drained

2 apples, Granny Smith are best, cored and finely chopped

2 hard boiled eggs, peeled and chopped

1/2 medium onion, peeled and finely chopped

1/3 cup celery, chopped

2 Tablespoons dill relish

1 Tablespoon prepared mustard

1 cup mayonnaise, less if you prefer a drier consistency

4 large, whole sweet peppers, cleaned, with caps and seeds removed

In a large bowl, combine all of the ingredients except for the peppers. Cover the tuna salad bowl tightly with plastic wrap and pop into the refrigerator.

Place the patted dry and hollowed-out peppers in a plastic or mesh bag. Leave the bag open/unsealed and store in the produce drawer of the refrigerator up to two days.

When ready to serve, simply spoon equal amounts of tuna into each pepper. Garnish with chopped tomatoes, minced onions, and/or a sprinkle of paprika.

>Cleaned, scooped-out tomatoes are a nice alternative to the peppers. Just add the tomato innards to the tuna mixture, reducing the amount of mayo as the consistency indicates.

>Tuna, like chicken salad, meatloaf, and most casseroles, is an excellent disguise for additional veggies in small quantities. Finely chopped yellow squash, shredded carrots, even riced, cooked cauliflower can be stirred into many dishes to add nutrients, fiber, and mild flavor. Just be wary of overdoing it. No one likes carrot salad with a touch of tuna!

Chicken Can Do

This is a pseudo-chicken and dumplings recipe. One of the lovely things about the real dish is the inclusion of chicken fat for flavor. But if you have canned chicken on hand, this recipe works quite well when you need a good meal in a hurry.

1 can cream of chicken soup (cream of nearly anything soup will work)

2 cups water or broth or white wine, or a combination

2 cans cooked chicken, well drained and shredded

1 bag frozen veggies (Peas and carrots are traditional, but choose any chopped up veggies you'd like.)

1 can mushrooms, slices or bits and pieces, drained and chopped

1/4 cup cocktail onions (or pearl onions), drained and chopped

1 teaspoon thyme

1 teaspoon oregano
1/2 teaspoon sage

Dumplings
2 cups baking mix: Jiffy, Bisquick, homemade, etc.
2/3 milk

In a large pot, whisk together the canned soup and the liquid of your choice. When well blended, add the remaining ingredients (Not the baking mix or milk, of course), and stir together.

Heat over medium high heat until bubbling. Stir often and feel free to add more liquid if necessary.

In a separate bowl, combine the baking mix and the milk. Do not over mix or the dumplings will fall apart. Just bring the ingredients together.

When the chicken mixture is simmering in the pot, drop the dough into it by the spoonful. Do not crowd the dumplings, or drop them on top of one another. Do not boil.

Cook the dumplings 10 minutes in the uncovered pot. Do not stir, or you will end up with the dough spread throughout your chicken.

Cover the pot and cook for 10 minutes more with the lid on. Do not peek. The dumplings need that heat and steam and liquid to cook properly.

After the additional 10 minutes, remove the lid and insert a toothpick into a dumpling. If it comes out clean, the you are ready to eat! If it is doughy, then cook the dumplings for another 2 – 5 minutes.

Fishing for Compliments

Some recipes are so easy, so reliable, and so well received that they become as much a part of your kitchen as the pots and pans. This is one of those recipes.

   Frozen fish fillet of your choice
   Milk or heavy cream
   White wine, optional
   Dried or fresh rosemary or dill

   Preheat the oven to 350*
   Line a baking pan with parchment (preferred) or aluminum foil. Place the fish on the prepared pan, pour about 1/2 cup of total liquid over each fillet. Season with herbs.

Fold the parchment or foil over the fillet(s) snugly, and place in oven. Bake for 20 minutes, testing for doneness by its internal temperature (140*-145*) and/or flakiness and opaqueness. Another option is to cook for 10 minutes per inch, until it reaches 145*

Remove cooked fresh herbs before serving.

>Consider pouring the excess liquid over steamed rice.

>This recipe can be used for frozen chicken, as well. Just choose boneless, skinless chicken fillets, tenders or breasts and cook until it reaches 165* internal temperature.

CRAVING CORNBREAD

A dreadfully cold evening, a fresh cup of coffee, and a plate of sizzling, hot cornbread, straight from the cast iron pan slathered with homemade butter is something to be experienced at least once in life. But in the meantime, these little wonders can satisfy that need for home sweet home.

Cornbread on the Stove
2 cups self-rising cornmeal
1 /12 – 2 cups water, or milk if you prefer
Butter or vegetable oil for frying
Large skillet

In a large bowl, stir the liquid into the cornmeal until the mixture resembles cake batter.

Put a little oil into the 12" skillet and heat on medium to medium-high. You want the pan to be hot enough to cook quickly to prevent the oil from soaking into the batter, but not so hot that it burns the outside before cooking through.

Very carefully, ladle the entire mixture into the warmed skillet, and cook until the edges brown, about 1 1/2 to 2 minutes. Test for doneness by poking a toothpick into the center. (If you prefer individual cakes rather than one larger circle of 'bread', simply cook like pancakes.)

Gently flip the bread and continue cooking, about 2 minutes more.

Place on paper towels to drain and eat hot. These are good with molasses, honey, or a dab of sour cream!

>If you have leftover cooked sausage, crispy bacon, cooked pinto, black, or other beans, sautéed veggies, etc., you can mix those ingredients into the batter, or top the prepared cornbread for a little variety.

DESSERTS

Yo-Gurt to Like This Banana Split

Do you love banana splits, but want a quick and healthier option? This is a really good substitute.

1 banana
Yogurt (plain Greek, vanilla Greek, flavored varieties)
1 generous handful each: frozen blueberries, frozen strawberries, frozen blackberries (or fruits of your choice)
Chocolate (syrup, grated, broken up candy bars, etc.)
Nuts, raw or roasted
Whipped cream (or whipped and sweetened yogurt)

Simply split the banana in half and place in a bowl. Drop spoonfuls of yogurt on top. Scatter berries over the yogurt, either all together, or in sections like traditional banana splits.

Cover the fruit with any chocolate of your choice, then evenly distribute the nuts before topping with the whipped cream or yogurt.

>Frozen fruit is best, but fresh fruits work well, too. You could also pop the yogurt in the freezer before making to more closely resemble ice cream.

What Cookies?

This is one of those recipes that you really shouldn't make on your own. These little no-bake cookies simply disappear, seemingly on their own! Remember, if asked where the cookies went, you can simply call them by their name.

   3/4 cup butter, soft
   1 cup brown sugar, firmly packed
   1 teaspoon vanilla
   2 cups quick rolled oats
   1/2 cup coconut and/or chopped nuts, optional
   Jam, jelly, preserves of your choice

Beat butter until creamy, add sugar and vanilla and blend until smooth. Stir in oats and optional coconut/nuts until well blended. The dough will be a little sticky and quite stiff.

Chill dough until it can be easily handled. Roll into 1" balls. Gently press center of each ball with your thumb, then fill with the jam or jelly of your choice. Or skip the jam-filling step and drizzle with chocolate or roll in chopped nuts.

If there are any left, store in a sealed container in the fridge. Hidden beneath the package of kale. In the back.

Par-Fancy and Par-Fast

Use up any stale cookies, cake, even donuts, in this quick and delicious parfait!

1 3-ounce package cream cheese, softened
2 packages (4 serving size) instant pudding (lemon and/or vanilla work best)
1 cup plain yogurt (or sour cream for a pleasantly tart base)
2 1/2 cups milk
2 cups crushed, chopped, odds and ends of cookies OR day old cake, OR stale doughnuts

In a large bowl, whip the cream cheese before adding the dry instant pudding mix. When well blended, add the yogurt/sour cream and blend again. Slowly add the milk, mixing until the pudding is smooth.

Use tall glasses or actual parfait dishes, and alternate layers of pudding and fillings (cake, cookies, etc.), beginning and ending with pudding.

>Another option is to forego the baked goods and use fresh or frozen berries. Or make it even better by layering pudding, berries, cake and then pudding again.

Thanks for the Cake

This is a wonderful recipe to have on hand during the fall holidays. During such a busy time of year, even those folks who love to bake sometimes need a speedy option when asked to bake "just a little something" for work or family.

1 box cake mix, spice is the best, or add pumpkin pie spices to yellow cake mix
1 15-ounce can plain canned pumpkin
2 eggs

Preheat the oven to 350*
Prepare a 9x13 pan with nonstick baking spray (I always use Baker's Joy.)
In a large bowl, combine all three ingredients. An electric mixer is really good at blending thoroughly.

>You might want to add a couple teaspoons of pumpkin pie spice and a dash of pepper to the mixture for added pizazz. Just be sure to thoroughly incorporate the spices into the batter.

Pour batter into prepared pan and bake 20-25 minutes. Test by putting a toothpick or knife into the center of the cake. If it comes out clean, the cake is done. If you see any trace of batter, put it back in the oven for another 3-5 minutes and test again.

Right before serving, top with dollops of commercial or homemade sweetened whipped cream. Sprinkle with pumpkin pie spice.

Yo-PB-Freeze

So you just found out you're having company for dinner in a few hours, and it is way too hot to even think of using the oven. This dessert can be made just a little ahead of time without a lot of effort. Mix it up, toss it in the freezer, and scoop it out. Whew!

2 cups vanilla Greek yogurt
1/2 cup maple syrup (other liquid sweeteners can be used: honey, agave, etc.)
1/2 cup nut butter, peanut, almond, cashew, etc.
2 teaspoons vanilla

In a metal mixing bowl, beat together the yogurt, syrup, nut butter and vanilla until well blended and smooth.

Place the bowl into the freezer for a couple of hours, or overnight. The longer it freezes, the harder it will be.

Serve plain or top with sliced bananas, drizzle with chocolate syrup, and/or add a dollop of whipped cream.

Oh, Sweet Milquetoast

You may recall the breakfast recipe for Mighty Milquetoast. Well, this is a variation that is just as easy to put together, but includes such delights as sugar and cinnamon and always lovely vanilla extract.

  2 slices best quality bread
  Butter
  2 cups whole milk or heavy cream, or a blend
  2 teaspoons vanilla extract
  1 teaspoon cinnamon
  2 teaspoons sugar

While toasting the bread to a lovely golden brown, gently heat the milk over low heat in a saucepan on the stove. Add the vanilla, cinnamon and sugar. Stir frequently and do not allow it to scorch.

When the toast is done, spread generously with butter, cut into pieces, and place in a bowl. Cover with warmed milk and sprinkle with just a little more cinnamon and/or sugar. Serve immediately.

It's similar to bread pudding without the long oven time. A warming and comforting dish after an afternoon spent making snow angels!

S'mores Weather

While watching the leaves fall, after building a snow fort, or when nursing a sunburn, there is no better time for a pan of s'mores than right now!

1 1/2 cups chocolate chips (or 10 ounces of baking chocolate, broken into pieces)
1 Tablespoon milk
12 full sized marshmallows
Graham crackers, cookies, bears, etc.

Generously butter an oven safe 8x8 pan. Set aside.
Preheat the oven to 425*
In a large microwave safe bowl, stir together the chocolate and milk. Microwave for 2 – 3 minutes at a time, stirring often to check for melting. Chocolate rarely looks like it's melting until it is too late and has burned.

Once the mixture has completely melted, stir until smooth and pour into the bottom of the prepared pan. Top with the marshmallows and pop into the hot oven.

Watch very closely. Those marshmallows should be melted and a lovely golden color in about 4-6 minutes.

Remove from the oven carefully since the sticky marshmallows will be seriously hot. Serve with graham-anything and enjoy!

Beyond Pudding

This lovely dessert can be eaten as a pudding, used as a pie filling, or served as a luscious dip for cookies and fruits. It is decadent. And if you make it before starting to cook dinner, it can chill while you eat and be ready right on time!

1 5-ounce package instant dry pudding mix of your choice: French vanilla, cheesecake, lemon, chocolate, etc.

Dash of salt to cut the sweetness and brighten the flavor. A squeeze of lemon juice works, too.

2 cups cold milk

1 generous Tablespoon vanilla extract, or use half vanilla extract and half another relevant flavor

1 14-ounce can sweetened condensed milk (not evaporated milk!)

1 1/2 cups whipped cream: homemade or commercial

In a large bowl, use an electric mixer to combine the pudding mix and milk.

Once the pudding mix is completely incorporated into the milk, add the vanilla and sweetened condensed milk.

Beat on high until all of the ingredients are fully blended and smooth.

Gently fold in the whipped cream until you can no longer see streaks of white. If you opt to stir the whipped cream in, or use the mixer for this step, your pudding will taste good, but will not be nearly as airy or lovely as if you took the time to fold it in. I have to admit that I am not a fan of folding, but the results are actually worth it!

Now you can choose how you'd like to serve it:

- Spoon the pudding into separate dishes to chill. Serve with a dollop of whipped cream and/or a sprig of mint, or a piece of candied lemon peel – ooh la lah.

- Pour the pudding into a graham cracker pie shell. Smooth the top and cover before chilling.

- Cover and chill before spooning into a serving bowl along with a tray of raw fruit (strawberries, frozen banana slices, etc.) and/or cookies.

>This is a very sweet pudding, so you might want to tone that sweetness down by reserving 2 Tablespoons of the sweetened condensed milk called for above, and use it in your coffee, drizzle it over cake, or add melted dark chocolate to it for a ultra-rich ice cream topping.

Snap Your Fingers Fudge

With just two ingredients and a freezer, you have everything you need to create a rich dessert from scratch. Did I mention it takes less than 15 minutes to complete?

- 1/2 cup peanut butter (or other nut butter)
- 1/4 cup maple syrup

In a medium bowl, whisk the PB and the syrup together until they are well blended. Pour into a parchment-lined 8x8 pan. Top with another sheet of parchment and flatten the mixture out using your hands. Make the fudge as level as possible.

Freeze for 10 minutes. Remove, cut and serve!

So good and so fast!

Chip-A-Roo Bars

This layered dessert has a little something for everyone: Crispy rice cereal, butterscotch goodness, and yes, you guessed it, that always tasty chocolate! Oh, and peanut butter, too!

 1 cup sugar
 1 cup light corn syrup
 1 cup peanut butter, smooth or chunky
 6 cups crispy rice cereal
 1 1/2 cups chocolate chips
 1 cup butterscotch chips (or peanut butter, if you prefer)

Generously butter a 9x13 pan. Set aside.
In a heavy 3-quart pan, over medium heat, cook the sugar and corn syrup until it boils.

Remove the pan from the heat and completely stir in the peanut butter. Pour this mixture into a large, heat proof bowl, then stir in the rice cereal about a cup at a time. Make sure the cereal is well coated.

Press this mixture into the prepared pan.

Next, place the chips (chocolate, butterscotch, peanut, etc.) in a microwave safe bowl and melt at a low setting in 1 or 2 minute intervals. Stir between each period because you will not be able to tell how soft the chips have gotten by simply looking at them.

When completely melted and well blended, spread the melted chips over the pressed cereal mixture in the pan. Eat while still warm or chill until the chocolate is firm and enjoy!

Store in an airtight container for three to five days.

Nothing New No-Bakes

You may have made these a million times, but why not include this favorite recipe that can be made any time of the day or night and includes all of the major food groups: chocolate!?

1 stick butter
2 cups sugar
1/2 cup milk
1/4 cup cocoa
1/2 cup peanut butter
2 teaspoons vanilla
3 cups oats (Old fashioned oats for a chewier cookie, Quick oats for a meltier cookie)
A timer

Line two baking sheets with parchment paper (or foil or waxed paper). Set aside.

>Premeasure everything because we are basically making a candy and it will be important to work steadily.

In a large, heavy-bottomed pan, combine the butter, milk, sugar, and cocoa. Over medium heat, stirring constantly, watch for the butter to melt and everything to be combined and smooth. You might want to use a whisk instead of a spoon.

Bring this mixture to a rolling boil for exactly 60 seconds. Seriously. This will allow the sugar crystals to dissolve and will help the cookies set properly. Stir often, but not rapidly or constantly. The mixture needs to cook through without added air (rapid stirring) or a lowered temperature (constant stirring).

Remove from the heat and mix in the peanut butter and the vanilla immediately. Stir until the peanut butter is completely incorporated into the hot mixture. It is important to do this fairly quickly so the end result won't be dry cookies.

Next, stir in the oats, about a cup at a time, being sure to coat all of the oats with the PB/cocoa blend. You don't want to bite into a pocket of dry oats later!

Drop by the spoonful (or use a small scoop) onto the prepared pans. Allow to cool – if you can!

>You can also pour the entire concoction into a 9x13 pan, lined with parchment or buttered well. This method is faster than scooping out individual cookies, but it will require a longer cooling time, and you will have to be

careful to store it air-tight since the larger surface area is more likely to dry out quickly.

Assuming there are any leftovers, you can store these in an airtight container for a week. You can freeze them, too. Just wait until they have completely cooled before putting them into freezer-proof containers, and allow the cookies to come to room temperature before serving. Or keep partially frozen, chop and use as a topping for ice cream!

Recipes for Recipes

Although you may choose to buy premade mixtures, stirring up a batch of your own tasty concoctions takes just a few minutes. By making your own, you can also adjust the spiciness, add favorite flavors, or even skip certain ingredients entirely.

<u>Italian Seasoning</u>
3 tablespoons oregano
2 Tablespoons basil
2 Tablespoons parsley
1 Tablespoon thyme
1 Tablespoon onion
1 Tablespoon garlic powder
1 teaspoon marjoram
1 teaspoon dried rosemary

Mix all of these ingredients together and store in an airtight jar. This recipe can be easily doubled or tripled.

Salt Substitute

1 1/2 teaspoons cayenne pepper
1 Tablespoon black pepper
1 Tablespoon dry mustard
3-4 Tablespoons garlic powder
2 Tablespoons onion powder
1 Tablespoon marjoram
1 Tablespoon basil
1 Tablespoon savory
1 Tablespoon sage
1 Tablespoon thyme
1 Tablespoon parsley
1 Tablespoon mace, or to taste
2 Tablespoons dried lemon zest (or the zest from one lemon)

Mix all of the ingredients together in a bowl and store in an airtight container. This can be used instead of salt, or as additional seasoning for practically any savory food.

Baking Mix

1 cup all-purpose flour
1 1/2 teaspoon baking powder
1/8 teaspoon salt,
1 Tablespoon butter

Stir the dry ingredients together before cutting the butter into the mixture. You can substitute the flour, baking powder and salt with one cup self-rising flour.

Freeze to store.

A Note to the Reader

Thank you for purchasing this cookbook. I hope you have enjoyed using it as much as I have enjoyed putting it together for you!

Please consider leaving a review on Amazon, Goodreads, etc. As a newly published writer, I would certainly appreciate it.

And take a moment to look for my other books:

Stories for Every Season:
Creative Writing Prompts to Inspire and Encourage the Writer Within

Ready to Wear:
A Comfortable Collection of Poetry to Slip Into Every Day

But Wait, There's More ...

Sign up to learn about exclusive promotions, special events, and in-person author visits. Easily purchase current titles online and be the first to know where and when all of Susan's newest books will be available.

It's as easy as visiting:

www.SusanRayWriter.com

or by scanning this QR code with your phone!

Made in the USA
Columbia, SC
02 November 2024